# Writing for College History
## A Short Handbook

**Robert M. Frakes**

*Clarion University*

HOUGHTON MIFFLIN COMPANY    BOSTON   NEW YORK

Editor-in-Chief: Jean L. Woy
Sponsoring Editor: Sally Constable
Development Editor: Leah R. Strauss
Associate Project Editor: Reba Libby
Editorial Assistant: Kendra Johnson
Production/Design Coordinator: Bethany Schlegel
Senior Manufacturing Coordinator: Marie Barnes
Senior Marketing Manager: Sandra McGuire

Cover Image: Saul Steinberg, Shadows 1972 (detail) Wood, metal, staples, and cloth, with graphite, gouache, colored-pencils, and rubber stamp on panel, 18 x 24 inches. ©2002 The Saul Steinberg Foundation/Artists Rights Society (ARS), New York.

Printed in the U.S.A.

Library of Congress Control Number: 2002109450

ISBN: 0–618–30603–X

123456789-QUF-05 04 03

# Table of Contents

# Appendices

# Introduction

After more than 15 years of reading and grading student essays in a variety of teaching environments (high school, community college, regional state university, and research university), I have come to the conclusion that many students need a handbook to aid their writing for college-level history classes. The following collection of instructions has been developed on the basis of my experience together with the aid of college classes which have acted as "laboratories" for writing. It is my aim that students who follow the advice laid out in these pages will not only improve their written expression in college history classes, but also in other venues of their lives.

As you read through this handbook, you will notice it is built from the "ground up." The first chapter shows how to compose short writing assignments like the sentence, the paragraph, the journal assignment, and the letter assignment. The next chapter deals with the in-class essay. Subsequent chapters give "nuts and bolts" advice on how to write different types of papers. Along the way, I give some examples of effective and ineffective writing, modeled on (although not copied from) some of the work I have received from the approximately 5,000 students I have taught and graded since 1983. By examining these samples, and the accompanying comments, you will be able to learn important ground rules for writing various assignments. Of course, you will want to pay careful attention to any instructions or hints given by your instructor. Most instructors would agree that the ideal essay or paper today should be clear and well structured and still argue a point (and at some level a creative one). The approach presented in this handbook should be useful not just for history classes, but should also translate to college-level courses in English, Political Science, Anthropology, and Philosophy. I have aimed this handbook toward a broad audience including students at community colleges, regional state universities, small liberal arts college, and even research universities. I would like to thank Dr. David Toye (of Northeast State Technical Community College), Dr. George Frakes (emeritus of Santa Barbara City College), Professor Katherine Sibley (of St. Joseph's University), Drs. Todd Pfannestiel and Janet Knepper (of the History and English Departments, respectively, of Clarion University), Anthony Maccarella (my high school teaching consultant at Parsippany Hills High School), and Mary Dougherty of Houghton Mifflin Company for their comments and suggestions. I also thank Susan and Catherine Frakes for once again reading several drafts and Hannah and Lilith for their patience. I encourage students to work through this handbook carefully, reflect on their own writing, and also reflect on other writing that they encounter throughout their lives.

# CHAPTER 1
## Short Writing Assignments

This chapter will lead the student through various kinds of short writing assignments starting with the sentence and progressing to the paragraph, the journal, and the letter. Some of these are typically given as in-class writing assignments and others may be required as homework. As you read through the sections, please pay particular attention to the examples and try to learn the ropes of what makes an effective written response.

## 1.1    The Sentence

All students should be familiar with the sentence as the smallest building block of writing. Typically defined as "a complete thought," the sentence should be composed of, minimally, a subject, a verb, and usually an object. Sentences that don't contain the minimum ingredients are classified as "sentence fragments," and those that are so overly-long that they contain more than one complete thought are "run-on" sentences.

### Examples of Good and Bad Sentences

I use the terms "good" and "bad" throughout this handbook. While "effective" and "ineffective" might be more sensitive equivalents to "good" and "bad," it is important to remember that you are trying to write clearly and to earn a good grade in your history course.

*Alexander the Great conquered Egypt around 334 B.C.* (Subject: Alexander; Verb: conquered; Direct Object: Egypt. The approximate date gives additional information.)

*One city state many gods around important.* (This sentence is garbled because of its lack of a verb. I presume the student meant to insert the verb "had," although I'm still a little unclear on the word "important" tacked at the end. Perhaps the sentence was supposed to convey: *One city state had many gods and believed they were very important.* On the other hand, maybe the sentence should have read: *It is very important that one city state had many gods.*)

*Theodore Roosevelt were president of the United States in 1900.* (This sentence suffers from a lack of subject-verb agreement. A singular subject must have a verb form in the singular; a plural subject should use a plural verb form.)

You can see why clear sentence structure is critical. While an instructor may be generous and try to decipher the intended meaning of your words, many instructors will not and, in fact, will feel it is part of their job to teach you to write clearly. Instructors often hold to the adage: "Fuzzy writing indicates fuzzy thinking."

## 1.2    The Sentence as a Building Block

While instructors may require you to write a sentence in response to a question on an examination, you will more likely be required to use sentences in larger units of writing such as an identification paragraph, an essay, a book review, or a paper. In any of these units, you should effectively use various kinds of sentences such as a topic sentence (to introduce the paragraph or argument), sentences developing examples and evidence (to show your knowledge of a subject or to build an argument), transition sentences (to shift from one topic to another), and a concluding sentence (to state the significance of what you are writing).

### Examples of Various Kinds of Sentences

In the following examples, determine if the sentences are playing the role of a topic sentence, a developing sentence, a transition sentence, or a concluding sentence.

*There are several key reasons why the Romans were able to conquer the Mediterranean World.* (This topic sentence is setting up a paragraph, essay, or paper.)

*Another critical reason for the expansion of Christianity is the organization of a hierarchy in the early Church.* (This topic sentence introduces a paragraph within an essay.)

*While the Romans lost 50,000 troops at the Battle of Cannae in 216 B.C., they were able to go on to win the war because of their enormous manpower reserves.* (This sentence develops an example as part of a greater argument.)

*In his novel* Babbitt, *Sinclair Lewis satirizes the middle class values of mid-twentieth century America.* (This sentence develops primary source evidence as part of a greater argument.)

*In addition to taxation issues, the ideology of Enlightenment thinkers such as John Locke provided further drive for revolutionary change.* (This sentence marks a transition from the treatment of one example to another.)

*Although there were many reasons for Rome's expansion, the Roman concept of abstract citizenship would go on to influence many important future states, including the United States.* (This sentence concludes a paragraph or essay.)

## 1.3    The Paragraph

A paragraph is a group of sentences (at least two), developing a central idea. Usually you start with a topic (or introductory) sentence, write several sentences developing different examples, and end with a concluding sentence. You will probably be assigned to write paragraphs either as "identification paragraphs" or as building blocks of essays (or both).

## 1.4    The History Identification Paragraph

A standard part of examinations in many college history courses throughout the United States is the "identification paragraph." Rather than simply requiring students to memorize events and respond to a list, the identification paragraph (sometimes called by its abbreviation "I. D.") requires the student to give not only some critical historical information, but also to interpret that information.

*[handwritten margin note:] ✱ CRITICAL INFO + INTERPRETATION*

Although instructors are sometimes loath to explain what should be the "proper" length, try to aim for around four to five sentences. Keep in mind that the identification paragraph should be able to stand alone, with an introductory sentence, supporting sentences in a logical order, and a concluding sentence. A handy guide to remembering what should be addressed in a history I. D. paragraph are the 5 Ws:

**QUESTIONS**

Who?

What?

Where?

When?

and So What? (or What is the historical significance of the person, place, or event?)

Let's walk through an example. Usually the instructor will pick critical names of people, events, or developments that have been topics of the instructor's lectures. For our example, we'll write a history identification paragraph on ziggurats (a classic exam subject for an Early Western or World Civilization class).

Now, if you were constructing an I. D. paragraph on ziggurats you would want to address the 5 W's as previously mentioned.

You could accomplish this task in a minimum of about four sentences. After a quick review of your notes, you might easily come up with:

What = a temple

Where = Mesopotamia

This information could be the core of your introductory first sentence: *A ziggurat was a temple in ancient Mesopotamia.* So far, so good.

How about When? You might know that ziggurats existed in Mesopotamia for centuries. So, a safe dating would be to give a range: *A ziggurat was a temple in ancient Mesopotamia. Mesopotamians worshipped at ziggurats for centuries from c. 3000 B.C.E–1000 B.C.E.*

The <u>Who</u> aspect of this particular identification paragraph is a little more complicated. Since we cannot easily come up with an individual associated with a ziggurat, we can instead use an official, such as the priest-kings who performed sacrifices there. So, now we have a paragraph in progress that reads:

*A ziggurat was a temple in ancient Mesopotamia. Mesopotamians worshipped at ziggurats for centuries from c. 3000 B.C.E.–1000 B.C.E. The priest-kings of Mesopotamian cities ruled from the ziggurats and performed sacrifices there.*

Thus far, we have covered <u>Who</u>, <u>What</u>, <u>Where</u>, and <u>When</u> and so have four of the five essential points. Since this covers 80%, our I. D. paragraph to this point might realistically be given the grade of "B." To complete it, we need to answer <u>So What</u>—the historical significance part. It is useful to think of this as the concluding sentence of your paragraph. A quick and simple way to set up the sentence is to write: *Ziggurats are historically significant because….*

This is where you have to do some interpretation. Ultimately, you will want to tie the specific example of ziggurats to the larger general historical view of the period (in this case, the ancient Near East). If you are taking an early Western or World Civilization course, you probably will have noticed that your textbook and instructor have stressed the religious nature of society in the ancient Near East. This would fit very well with your identification paragraph on ziggurats. So, in the end, your I. D. paragraph might read:

*A ziggurat was a temple in ancient Mesopotamia. Mesopotamians worshipped at ziggurats for centuries from c. 3000 B.C.E.–1000 B.C.E. The priest-kings of Mesopotamian cities ruled from the ziggurats and performed sacrifices there. Ziggurats are historically significant because they show the central role religion had in ancient Mesopotamia and in the ancient Near East.*

## Time Budgeting for Identification Paragraphs

A critical point to keep in mind when you are taking in-class written examinations is how much time you have available. If you are taking a standard Monday/Wednesday/Friday class, you might have 50 minutes available for the examination. (Likewise, you might have 75 minutes if it is a Tuesday/Thursday class.) Hypothetically, you might be asked to compose three identification paragraphs and one essay in 50 minutes. If that is the case, you should plan out beforehand how much time you should devote to each section of the exam. Be sure to ask your instructor ahead of time about how the exam will be structured.

Although the amount of time for an adequate response varies from instructor to instructor, five minutes should provide enough time to develop the core of an identification paragraph. This would give you one minute to organize your thoughts and then a minute on each sentence if you were to write four sentences. If you did indeed have 50 minutes for the exam and had to write three I. D.'s and an essay, you would then spend 15 minutes on the I. D.'s and have 35 minutes left for the essay. Train yourself to immediately budget the time needed for the different parts of the exam. Practice cracking out an I. D. in five minutes.

Since that is just one scenario, ask your instructor how long you should aim to spend on each part of the test. Ideally, you would ask this question a week before the test so that you could use the information when studying. Most importantly, wear a watch and bring extra pens and pencils!

### Examples of Good and Bad Identification Paragraphs

The following are some examples of identification paragraphs for lower-division introductory history courses (Western, World, and U.S.). Regardless of the course you are taking, it will be useful for you to examine these samples from a technical point of view. As you read through the examples, try to evaluate them in terms of the guidelines you have read. Do they have at least three sentences? Do they address "Who, What, Where, When, and Historical Significance"? Do they have complete sentences?

**Identification Paragraph #1: <u>Ziggurat</u>**. *A ziggurat was a temple in ancient society. Ziggurats were very important in ancient nations.*

**Comments:** This I. D. paragraph defines "what" the ziggurat was, but that is about it. It needs the "where" (Mesopotamia), "when" (c. 3000 B.C.E.), "who" (the priest-kings who conducted sacrifices, issued laws, and collected taxes here), and "historical significance" (showing the central role of religion in ancient Mesopotamian society or something to that effect).

**Identification Paragraph # 2:** <u>Pharaoh</u> *This was a king of a town or municipality or borough in olden times. He was a priest. There was one in each town in Asia. He was in charge of sacrifices and taking care of widows and orphans.*

**Comments:** This paragraph is not only lacking information, it contains misinformation. While a pharaoh was a monarch and so a type of "king," he was in charge of the Kingdom of Egypt, not a city-state "in Asia." There was not a pharaoh in every "town, municipality, or borough," but one for the entire kingdom. Also, the student does not give even an approximate date, just "olden times." Again, the student needs to go through the check list of who, what, where, when, and historical significance.

**Identification Paragraph #3:** <u>Neolithic Revolution</u> *The Neolithic Revolution, or "New Stone Age," took place c. 10,000 B.C.E. During this development early humans shifted from hunting and gathering to agriculture as their economic basis. This happened at various places, probably simultaneously, including the Fertile Crescent, West Africa, and India. Agriculture is important because it created a surplus of food and allowed populations to rise. It also freed 10% of the population from food production and this allowed for specialization of labor. This led to the creation of towns and to government.*

**Comments:** This I. D. paragraph is quite good. The author deals with "who, what, where, when," and even historical significance. In comparison to the preceding two examples, an instructor would probably quickly give it an "A." The one flaw (and again this would be minor) is that the author jumps to the creation of government at the end of the paragraph without directly spelling out the connection to agriculture (surplus, taxes, war).

**Identification Paragraph #4: <u>Articles of Confederation</u>** *When the American Colonies were emerging as the winner of their revolution against Great Britain at the end of the 1770s, their leaders (such as John Hancock and Robert Morris) realized they needed to form some kind of unified government. They came up with the first Constitution of the United States of America called the "Articles of Confederation" (ratified in 1781). The articles provided for a common defense and foreign policy, but had a weak centralized executive and had trouble raising taxes to deal with debts incurred during the war of independence. This ultimately led to the writing of our current constitution in 1787 with a strong executive branch. George Washington was the first president under this second (and still existing) constitution.*

**Comments:** This is a solid identification paragraph. It deals with the five <u>W</u>s in a clear manner. The author could give a little more clarification on the problems of the Articles of Confederation to provide a clearer analysis of how such problems led to our current constitution.

**Identification Paragraph #5: <u>Charles Darwin</u>** *Charles Darwin was a rich Englishman of the 19th century who is famous for his books* Origin of Species *(1859) and the* Descent of Man *(1871). After studying theology, Darwin went on a voyage around the world on the H.M.S. Beagle and was impressed by the diversity of plant and animal life which led him to develop the "Theory of Evolution" in which he argued that plants and animals evolved over a long period of time and were affected by natural selection and the survival of the fittest. In the* Descent of Man *he argued that human beings also evolved over thousands of years from earlier forms. His theories are important because they conflicted with the traditional Biblical view presented at the beginning of the Book of Genesis that states that God created the world,* *plants, animals, and humans in the course of a week (in 4004 BC according to Bishop Ussher).*

**Comments:** This is clearly a very strong I. D. paragraph. The student not only effectively covers the five Ws, but also develops the examples and historical significance well. The second sentence is overly long and could have been split after "diversity of plant and animal life." One possible weakness in this paragraph is that the student may have spent more than the allotted time in composing it, potentially forfeiting time on other sections of the exam. Again, make sure you have enough total time to develop your identification paragraphs and the essay (or other parts of your exam) adequately.

### How to Review for Identification Paragraphs

Now you have an idea as to what you should be aiming for when you compose an identification paragraph. This knowledge alone should help you better prepare for an examination because it will allow you to sift through your notes and estimate what is likely to come up on the exam. Identification paragraph terms have to be somewhat specific, yet still able to be tied into a larger historical context. So, people, subjects, and dates such as "ziggurat, pharaoh, Constantine, Martin Luther, 1789, and Lenin" would all be potential I. D. paragraph terms for a Western Civilization or World Civilization class while "rivers, stone, and towns" would not. Likewise, "Stamp Act, Great Awakening, Dred Scott Decision, Brown vs. Board of Education, and New Deal" might be likely terms for a U.S. history survey course while "economy, religion, and America" would not. A useful exercise in preparing for an exam would be to review your lecture notes and try to come up with three potential I. D. terms for each lecture. Then look at the "master list" you have compiled and see if you are able to address the five Ws for each of your potential terms. If you cannot, it is time to review your notes and check your textbook.

## **1.5**    The Paragraph as a Building Block of the Essay

You have now learned the basics of the historical identification paragraph. The skills you learned here should translate well into developing paragraphs as building blocks of a multi-paragraph essay. While the next chapter will treat the topic of the essay in detail, keep in mind the basics of paragraph construction. (Ideally, write more than two sentences, including a topic sentence at the beginning, sentences developing examples and evidence in the middle, and a concluding sentence at the end.)

## **1.6**    The Journal as a Writing Assignment

Some instructors assign journal writing as part of the writing assignments for their history classes. Instructors design these journal assignments to be either reactions to readings or to lectures. Usually, students are supposed to be writing these reactions in their journals over the course of many weeks before turning them in to the instructor. The pedagogic idea behind journals is that they can offer an alternate writing environment to that of the exam and allow students to develop their writing skills in a less stressful way. Journals can also serve as a vehicle for students to develop creativity in their writing about history.

### **Tips for Writing Journal Entries**

The following tips are compiled from the author's experiences, those of students, and advice from colleagues.
a.   Ask the instructor what he or she really wants for journal entries. If you feel unsure after the explanation, meet with your instructor later during office hours and bring your first two entries to see if you are on the right track.
b.   Use concrete examples, not just generalizations.
c.   Don't wait until the last minute (i.e., the night before the deadline or the end of the semester) to write your journal. This creates an impossible situation for yourself in which you are desperately trying to make up for lost time. The in-

structor can read through "thin" responses where the development of thought in your analysis is unclear.

d.  Don't copy your friends' or classmates' journal entries. Their writing styles are probably different and you may well be caught by your instructor.

### An Example of a Journal Assignment

**Analyze the Declaration of Independence** *The Declaration of Independence that Thomas Jefferson and Benjamin Franklin wrote in 1776 was really important. It helped start the American Revolution and showed why North American colonists wanted to have their own country. It's got a lot of great lines in it like "All men are created equal." At the same time, though, there are some problems because some of the leaders of the American Revolution didn't really think all men were created equal because they believed in slavery. Many enslaved African Americans were not helped by the Declaration of Independence, nor were many Native Americans. It would take a long time, at least past the Civil War, before the Declaration's ideas really spread throughout the whole country.*

**Comments**: This is a sound enough entry in that it places the document under examination in chronological context, names the authors, cites a line, and ponders some significance. It is somewhat unpolished, but that can probably be overlooked since the student has begun to do some analysis and would be able to refine the writing if it were a more formal assignment.

## 1.7   The Letter as a Writing Assignment

A clever assignment given by some instructors, usually in lower-division classes, is to have students write a letter as if they are living in some different historical period (such as during the U.S. Civil War or in ancient Greece). Through such a letter, the student can show an understanding of the major issues of a historical period while being creative. The stimulation of creativity leads some students to investigate the period in greater detail.

## Tips for Writing Historical Letters

The following tips are collected from the author's experiences, those of students, and advice from colleagues:

a.  Ask the instructor what he or she really wants for the letter. The biggest problem with this assignment is when students exercise their creative juices but don't attend to any of the historical material.

b.  Make sure to include some specific dates, political context, economic and social context, and even environmental factors.

c.  Make sure that the "respondent" of your letter is clearly identified in terms of occupation, location, and connection to the "author" of the letter.

d.  Don't wait until the last minute (i.e., at the end of the semester) to write your letter.

e.  Try to make your letter creative and unique.

## Sample Letter

Imagine that you are fighting in the trenches in France during World War I. Write a letter to someone back home. Page 11 shows an example of such a letter.

**Comments:** This letter assignment demonstrates that the student has an understanding of the political events of World War I France as well as some feel for life in the trenches. The context is well established, as is the author's changing viewpoint since the beginning of the war. While the reader doesn't get much insight into Molly, there is an attempt to examine the changing role of women in England during the war.

*April 15, 1916*
*Sgt. John Hughes*
*The King's Own Manchester Volunteer Rifles*
*2nd Regiment, 3rd Co.*

*Miss Molly Sedgewick*
*14 Southeby Row*
*Manchester, England*

*Dearest Molly,*

*Spring has begun again and with it, the infernal mud. We live, eat, and fight knee deep in mire. In the bloody trenches some of my mates have caught trench foot and many are lousy. Across No Man's Land sits Jerry in his lines. When the barrage begins, we dive down deep. When it lifts we man the lines and fix bayonets—we only hope there will be no more mustard gas.*

*It seems like only yesterday that it was August of 1914 and we postponed our engagement so that I could sign up with my pals to join the Volunteer Rifles. Then we thought the war would be over by Christmas, and I would get my position back at the mill working the power loom. We could marry and look forward to buying a row house.*

*Most in the line feel the same way. We are starting to wonder what we are fighting for. Might Jerry be feeling the same way? Some are even talking of making an action against the bloody officers.*

*I know things must be hard on the home front with all the men gone and the women working in the factories. I only hope that this World War will end soon and I can come home.*

*Yours Fondly,*

*John*

## **1.8**   Conclusion: Clarity and Content

You have now encountered many varieties of shorter writing assignments. Keep in mind that clarity and content are important for all of them. Strive to write your compositions (whether I. D. paragraph, journal entry, or letter) in a way that will make them clear to the reader in terms of style and sentence structure. Make sure they have content that pertains to the assignment and the period under study.

# CHAPTER 2
## The In-Class Essay

As a standard part of most midterm and final examinations, instructors of rigorous college-level history courses usually require students to write an essay. In this written composition, the student should ideally show an overview of the material, argue a point, cite historical evidence and examples to back it up, and present the essay in a lucid, well-organized way.

This chapter will explain how to write an effective essay for an in-class examination (as opposed to a composition you work on outside of class). You will find advice on how to structure an outline for your response, how to use evidence, and how to formulate a thesis or argument. You will also encounter some examples of strong and weak essays on a variety of historical topics. When you read through these essays, try to evaluate what grade you would give them and why. Such reflection will help you build the technical skills to write your own effective in-class essays.

## 2.1   The Five-Paragraph (or more) Essay

The classic history essay is made up of at least five paragraphs, but may include more depending on the phrasing of the question. (Remember, by definition, a paragraph must have at least two sentences and will usually have more.) Your essay should have an introductory paragraph (in which you try to frame an argument and lay out the structure of your essay), body paragraphs (in which you support your argument by means of citing evidence—especially primary sources and historical examples such as events, people, and cultural institutions), and a concluding paragraph (where you hint at the long-term significance).

**Essay Structure and Outlining**

If you have at least five paragraphs in your essay, you must have at least three body paragraphs which develop core examples. A rough skeleton outline would look something like this:

I.   Introduction
   - Argument (traditionally called a "thesis") where you explain the main point of your essay
   - Explicit structure ("By examining examples such as X, Y, and Z...")

II.  Body Paragraph
   - Evidence and examples

III. Body Paragraph
   - Evidence and examples

IV.  Body Paragraph
   - Evidence and examples

V.   Conclusion
   - Significance

Whenever possible, try to use chronology as an organizing tool. That is, move from an earlier example to a later example. If, for instance, you are tracing the causes of a major event, or are trying to describe the most important values of a 2000-year period, choose a series of examples that supports your point and look at the examples in chronological order. Such an approach makes historical sense because earlier events often affect later events. Using chronological organization also makes you look well organized to the grader of the essay.

Students are naturally curious as to how many dates they should memorize for an exam. Using relative chronological order in an essay demonstrates an overview of the period. Working at least one date into each body paragraph shows that you have some firm historical pivots for your relative chronology.

Be sure to pick examples for your body paragraphs that actually pertain to your thesis (or argument) and to the question. You would be surprised at how many students wander off the topic (probably trying to show that they know something, at least). If an example doesn't clearly and easily pertain to the question, it is simpler and more effective not to make it one of your core examples.

Use a representative range of examples. If you are supposed to be looking at a period of 300 years, try to space out your examples in time and not have them all "clumped" together at the beginning or the end of the 300-year period.

Also, try to look at both sides of an issue. For instance, if you are looking at the causes of a war, whenever possible give examples of what is motivating both sides so your essay isn't skewed or biased. Or, if you are comparing and contrasting two cultures, try to give examples from both.

## 2.2   Primary Sources and Point of View

The best kind of ammunition to include in the body paragraphs of your in-class essay is primary source evidence. Primary sources are literary works (such as letters, laws, speeches, articles, and books) or material/ archaeological remains from the time period under examination. When possible, either cite the primary sources directly or at least allude to some examples (through a formula like "as can be seen in primary sources such as ..."). Primary sources are even more effective if you examine the point of view of the authors. Were they rich or poor, did they like a development or were they negatively biased against it? How might those circumstances color the way they see events?

## 2.3   Time Budgeting for Essays

Make sure you know beforehand how much time you will be given to write the essay and budget your time accordingly. If you are in a typical 50 minute class, you might have 30 or 35 minutes to write the essay (assuming you spend the first 15 to 20 minutes on identification paragraphs). If you are writing a classic five-paragraph essay, and if you spend five minutes planning a rough outline, you would have about five minutes per paragraph. Many, many essays that the author has graded have initial paragraphs that are huge and then two or three ending paragraphs the student desperately dashed through trying to finish before the end of the class period. Avoid that mistake by making a time plan for the exam in the first 10 seconds, budgeting your time throughout the exam, and checking your watch periodically.

**Organizational Exercises**

Try taking a practice run at a couple of essay questions in terms of organization. With the following questions, fill in the blank space with a major development from your history class. How many paragraphs would you write for these questions? Keep in mind that instructors use some common formats for essay questions in history classes.

1. "Trace the developments leading to ..." (a causation question)
2. "What are the most important events ..." (an overview of material question)
3. "What are the major sources for ..." (an overview of primary source material question)
4. "Analyze the following quotations. What do they tell you about changes during the period under examination?" (an analysis of primary sources and developments question)
5. "What is the better explanation, a or b ..." (a provocative interpretive question)

## 2.4   The Thesis

The best essays always have an argument. Indeed, a clear dividing line for instructors between a good essay and a fair to poor one is whether or not there is a clear thesis. Sometimes the essay question will help you frame your thesis, such as #5 in the preceding list which immediately demands an argument. More often, it will be up to the student to craft a thesis.

Sometimes you can make overview questions (such as #s 1–3 in the list) into argumentative essays by using a device such as "Although there are many sources for ..., only five clearly stand out." When you have a causation question (such as causes of a war or impact of a development), it will be up to you to frame the question. Again, you can demonstrate your knowledge by crafting a thesis stating that there are three major causes of the given war, for instance, or four major effects of a development. Then you can examine each of those causes or effects in a body paragraph of your essay and state in your conclusion which one might have been more influential than the others. Question #4 could be especially well suited for crafting a thesis if you can find a central theme that runs through the quotations.

A common occurrence for students is that they don't arrive at a clear thesis until they reach the end of writing their essay. In a way, this situation makes sense because the student has worked through the evidence and examples and now has reached an evaluation. If this happens to you and if you have enough time, revise your introduction and work in this clarified thesis. If you don't have enough time, it is better to write in this thesis as the last sentence of your conclusion than not to have it at all.

## Examples of Good and Bad Essays

The following sample essays are typical of some written by students in lower-division survey courses. As you read through these examples, try to evaluate them in terms of the guidelines you have read for essay writing. Review the following questions as a checklist (or rubric) you aim to complete in writing your own essay:

Do the essays have an introductory paragraph that states a thesis and lays out the structure? Do they have at least five paragraphs? Do the body paragraphs develop historical examples and primary source evidence to support the central argument? Do the essays have complete sentences? Are the overall arguments convincing? (Some instructors actually use explicit rubrics in grading essays. Be sure to ask your instructor if he or she does.)

**Essay #1** Question: Which was more important in the early societies we have examined thus far: technology or religion?

*Religion was the most important thing in the ancient societies. In every society of ancient times, religion was very important in ancient western civilization back then. It was more important than technology.*

*In the early societies sometimes older societies allowed other societies they met to continue worshipping the god they worshipped before. On the other hand, sometimes that didn't always happen with ancient peoples and gods then. It's sometimes different today, but not always.*

*There was at one time a time period of early history in ancient societies into which where there were more than one god sometimes. Indeed, moreover there were many in some and other countries might have different gods at the same time.*

*However, others believed in polytheism (which is a belief in many gods, poly means many in Greek). Some had two gods, also. This was another kind of religion in some city-states. One of the ancient societies even, on the other hand, believed in monotheism, which was a belief of religion where you had one and only one god (mono means "one and only one" in Greek).*

*Religion had a bigger role in the ancient societies of the past world then. Now technology is more important. Who knows what the future will hold?*

**Comments:** This essay has some severe problems. On the positive side, the student has a thesis in the introductory paragraph and is trying to have five paragraphs. The paragraphs are weak, however, because they are short and superficial and they don't cite any specific historical examples or citation of evidence. For instance, the first and second body paragraphs are very unclear as to what the student is referring (perhaps to the Persians with their tolerant religious policy and the Assyrians with their harsh one?). The last body paragraph is clearly trying to discuss monotheism. Here the student should mention the Hebrews and their scriptures, the Ten Commandments, etc. Another serious problem is the lack of any sense of chronology. The student should try to use relative chronological order going from the earliest example to later ones and also attempt to work a date into each body paragraph that ties to a specific example.

**Essay #2** Question: If you could choose only five events to explain Early Western History (from c. 10,000–500 B.C.E.) to a friend, which events would you choose and why?

*The five most important events of all time in Early Western History that I would explain to my friend are the Paleolithic Age, the Neolithic Age, the Stone Age, the Flint Age, the Copper Age, the Mesozoic Age, and the Steel Age. These are the most important ages in Early Western History and happened after the dinosaur ages.*

*The Paleolithic Age demonstrates different ways by which people hunted food. The Neolithic age, on the other hand, shows how people hunted. The Copper and Bronze ages show how people used metal for things as did the steel ages. Sometimes things changed, but other times they didn't.*

*These different ages are the most important events in Early Western History.*

**Comments:** This essay has several problems. Clearly, it doesn't have enough paragraphs to develop examples. Moreover, the author actually mentions seven "ages" in the introduction instead of five "events." There is an initial problem because an age (which is a very long period of time) is not an event (which is a single historical development). Looking at the question, it would appear that the essay should have seven paragraphs (an introductory paragraph, five body paragraphs developing **five** examples, and a conclusion). The student does have an introductory paragraph, but makes a conceptual mistake in so far as the Paleolithic and Neolithic Ages are both part of the Stone Age. Additionally, I have never heard of a "Flint Age," but apparently the student didn't either in so far as it is not developed. The Mesozoic Age must have crept in from another class (perhaps in the geology department).

The second paragraph, which should be a paragraph devoted to developing the Paleolithic Age as an example, instead presents a cursory overview of the importance of some of the periods (where the author makes some sweeping overgeneralizations and mistakes). The student should instead have mentioned examples and evidence from each period in a series of successive body paragraphs before ultimately writing a concluding paragraph.

**Essay #3** This is another example of a student's answer to the question in Essay #2.

*While many important events occurred in early history, during the period from 10,000 BCE to 500 BCE, there were some which were even more important than others. If I had to choose only five to explain to a friend, I would probably choose the Neolithic Revolution, the discovery of bronze, the creation of the chariot, the invention of the alphabet, and the development of iron technology because of the huge effect they had in changing history.*

*The "Neolithic Revolution" (i.e., the shift to agriculture) was invented c. 10,000 BCE. With agriculture as a food supply (as opposed to only hunting and gathering used in the preceding Paleolithic Age) populations rose and there was enough of a surplus of food to free up 10% of the population from food production to instead be involved in crafts, trade, the military, and government. However, according to Karl Marx, with the creation of agriculture came the concept of property and wealth. So along with the creation of agriculture came the creation of conflict. To defend against internal and external conflict (or crime and war), government was created to form the abstract state which had not existed in the Paleolithic age. This government maintained justice and provided defense.*

*The creation of efficient bronze technology took place c. 2000 BCE somewhere on the northern frontier of Mesopotamia (although there were earlier experiments that weren't as efficient). Bronze, an alloy of copper and tin, proved superior to copper (the previous metal of choice) because it was harder and thus better for weapons. Bronze was an expensive metal because tin was a scarce resource. In order to obtain tin, extensive trade networks had to be developed that stretched all the way from the Eastern Mediterranean to Cornwall (in England).*

*A major important development is the invention of the alphabet (c. 1000 BCE). While earlier writing systems had been pictographic or ideograms (such as Egyptian hieroglyphics or Mesopotamian cuneiform), these writing systems had a large number of characters and only the elite could have the leisure time to learn these older scripts. It was the great merchant people of the Phoenicians who developed a 22-symbol system of writing which allowed all members of their society to learn a form of written communication and aided their great mercantile activity throughout the Mediterranean world. So, the Phoenician creation of the alphabet allowed for mass literacy. This system would be subsequently adopted by the Greeks and the Romans. The Western alphabet today stems from that of the Romans, because of the influence of the Catholic Church.*

*The last example from the ancient world is the invention of efficient iron technology (c.1000 BCE) somewhere in Northern Mesopotamia (although a few earlier examples made from meteoric iron have been discovered). Because this new metal was so much more plentiful than bronze, it could equip much larger armies. The Assyrians were the first people to harness the effectiveness of iron technology and equip mass armies. This development allowed the Assyrians to expand and create the first large empire stretching from Mesopotamia to Egypt.*

*While many important events took place in Early Western History, the most significant were the Neolithic Revolution, the creation of efficient bronze technology, the invention of the alphabet, and the creation of efficient iron technology.*

**Comments:** This essay is clearly better than the previous examples. It has a clear structure, good examples, and some effective development. An unfortunate mistake is that the author forgot to develop example #3 (chariots). This kind of oversight does happen, so it is always a good idea to lay out your explicit structure in your introductory paragraph (which the author did), but then periodically refer back to it as you finish each body paragraph. It may be helpful to make a very rough outline on scratch paper or inside the front cover of your blue book before beginning your essay.

Aside from that, there are two more minor problems. The body paragraph on the invention of bronze technology seems underdeveloped in comparison with the others. The paragraph would have been more effective if the author alluded to a few major bronze age peoples (such as the Hittites, the New Kingdom of Egypt, and the Mycenaeans). This improvement could have been done simply by alluding to them through a formula such as "Some major societies who made use of this new bronze technology included X, Y, and Z."

Lastly, the conclusion is also a bit underdeveloped. The author basically restates the introduction. While it may be difficult in an essay question of this type to go further, you should, at least, avoid a one-sentence paragraph. Perhaps adding a final sentence such as "Without these critical developments, ancient societies would have been stuck either in the Paleolithic Age or at a very localized level" would show the long-running significance of these examples.

**Essay #4** Question: What caused the U.S. Civil War?

*There is no easy answer to the question of what caused the Civil War. Historians have debated (and probably will continue to debate) over economic, political, and social issues. However, three chief areas emerge after re-examination as the three biggest causes. They are 1) historical regional differences, 2) expansion, and 3) abolitionism.*

*The Northern and Southern colonies were always different in North America. The North (New England) was settled at first primarily by English settlers who wanted small farms or shops in cities like Boston. They believed in what scholars such as Max Weber call the "Puritan Work Ethic." Southern colonists were mostly Scotch-Irish settlers and wanted to mimic British aristocrats by having large plantations. Although there was some slavery in the North also early on, slaves worked especially well for agriculture in the South. When the Revolutionary War ended, North/South differences, especially slavery, were the biggest areas of concern in the framing of the Constitution. The Great Compromise and the 3/5th's Compromise both temporarily dealt with the difference between the North and South, but obviously didn't succeed in resolving the differences.*

*When the U.S. expanded during the age of "Manifest Destiny," there was a question as to whether slavery would be allowed in new states. Both the Missouri Compromise and the Compromise of 1850 dealt with this, but neither was permanently successful. The Southerners wanted slavery in the new lands because their use of cash crops like king cotton and sot weed (or tobacco) exhausted the soil and they needed new fresh lands. The North was industrializing and needed raw materials.*

*The North also had a growing movement against the "peculiar institution" of slavery called abolitionism. Led by figures such as William Lloyd Garrison and Harriet Tubman, and influenced by Harriet Beecher Stowe's novel* Uncle Tom's Cabin, *this movement became more and more influential in trying to not just stop slavery in the new states, but in trying to end it in the South itself.*

*A series of crises (Nat Turner's Rebellion, the Dred Scott Supreme Court decision, Bleeding Kansas, John Brown's Raid) fanned the flames, and none was successfully resolved. When Lincoln was elected in 1860, South Carolina seceded, followed by the deep South. Finally, Ft. Sumter was fired upon in 1861 and the Civil War began.*

**Comments:** The student clearly knows some things about American history leading up to the Civil War. The essay has a decent structure, cites some examples, and even provides three primary sources (the Constitution, *Uncle Tom's Cabin*, and the Supreme Court Dred Scott decision). However, the essay is not as strong as it could be. The thesis is serviceable, but weak. The first body paragraph could be developed more fully. The paragraph on expansion needs development for the Northern view.

Lastly, the shoe-horning of a series of crises in parenthesis in the concluding paragraph is not the most effective way to use and develop that evidence.

## 2.5   Conclusion: Studying for In-Class Essay Examinations

Knowing how to structure essay exams will help guide your ability to review for such tests. Remember to use major events and primary sources to support your essays. Try to make lists of the most critical developments, problems, and most important sources mentioned by your instructor. If a substantial amount of attention has been given to arguments between historians on the evaluation of a development, make sure you know the two sides and what the key evidence is.

Some students find it useful to construct hypothetical essay questions stressing the most critical elements of the instructor's lecture. If you make a list of four or five (and it helps to do this task with a friend from class), see if you could structure an outline with a thesis and evidence for each body paragraph for each potential question.

# CHAPTER 3
## The Five-Page Paper

A classic assignment for college history courses is the five-page paper. Unlike the in-class examination, students work on the topics of their papers at home (or in their dorm, apartment, or library) over the course of several weeks. When due, the student turns in five pages of typed (or word-processed) prose and hopes for the best. Keep in mind that a standard double-spaced 8½ × 11 inch page with normal margins of 1 inch from the top and bottom, and 1½ inch from right and left will yield about 250 words.

In Chapter 3 you will find advice on how to construct your thesis, how to structure your paper, and when and how to cite sources for a five-page paper. Like in earlier chapters, you will also find examples of effective and ineffective compositions. As you read through them, try to think about how you would grade the sample paper and why you would give it that grade. Once you start thinking about how your paper is graded, you are likely to become a better paper writer.

### 3.1  The Thesis of the Paper

Instructors will vary in how they set up their paper assignment, with some giving a list of topics from which the student chooses and others leaving the choice of topic wide open. Likewise, some instructors allow biographical papers, while others want papers based on events or on primary sources. Regardless of the choice of topic, instructors are generally more impressed by papers with a central argument in the introductory paragraph together with some kind of explicit structure (and, of course, the citation of several sources). So, even if you are writing on a person, event, or literary work, try to frame the paper as an argument. You can do this in several ways, and the topic, of course, will help determine this. A good approach is to find a central problem of interpretation.

Let's try an example. Suppose you want to write a paper on the Roman political leader Julius Caesar. Now you have to find a problem around which you can build an argument. A summary of his life would not be an argument and a tough instructor would lower your grade for it, no matter how encyclopedic it may be. Instead, you might want to offer an argument like "Why was Julius Caesar assassinated?" In the course of that paper, you will show that you know what happened in his life.

Let's look at a topic from American history. Suppose you had to write a paper on George Washington. You could choose to write a paper discussing the source of the story about George Washington and the cherry tree. This topic would force you to delve into sources about his life (and you might discover that the story comes from Parson Mason Wheems several years after Washington's death). Or, you could write a paper on the subject: "Was George Washington really the first President of the United States of America?" While this may seem like an obvious question at first, you might examine the leaders of the American states under the Articles of Confederation. You will discover that several men, including such worthies as John Hanson, held the title of president before Washington's term of office. Then you could refine the subject of your thesis to something like "First President of the United States of America: George Washington or John Hanson?" where you have sharpened your focus and, hopefully, intrigued the reader. Regardless of topic, try to find a meaty argument into which you can sink your teeth.

If you write a paper on a primary source, you will likewise want to make it into an argument. Let's say you are required to write a paper on Sophocles' tragedy *Antigone*. Instead of merely summarizing the play, you will want to hone in on a problem. Consider a topic such as why Sophocles chose to emphasize the play's moral to the audience of Athenian citizens, or discuss whether the portrayal of women in the play was supposed to represent historical reality.

As stated in the last chapter, it is fairly common to uncover your clarified thesis once you finish writing the rough draft of your paper. At this point you will definitely want to go back and revise your introductory paragraph and, quite likely, the topic sentences of several of your body paragraphs.

After laying out the thesis and structure in your introductory paragraph, you have different choices in how you might want to proceed. You could summarize the historical context or give a brief overview in a few paragraphs. Then you could determine some critical events or passages, analyze them, and offer a conclusion where you discuss the significance of your argument. You might want to skip the initial historical context section and work that material into the paragraphs in which you develop examples or passages from primary sources. **Regardless, keep in mind that you want to cite passages from primary sources to back up your argument. Without citation of sources, you will not be doing good historical writing, and your paper will surely not get a good grade.**

## 3.2    Sample Outlines

A key to writing a good paper is to have some kind of organization, which should be made clear to the reader in the first paragraph or two. Some writers like to organize very lengthy outlines, while others don't use them at all. However, it's important to keep in mind that you should know where you are going when you are writing.

Thus, you should have at least some kind of "basic" outline in mind. Let's try to outline some sample papers in response to different kinds of topics.

Question (a): Why was Julius Caesar assassinated?

I.    Introduction
II.   The last century of the Roman Republic (an overview)
III.  Julius Caesar's career
IV.   The assassination and the assassins

V.  Analysis (e.g., What was Caesar doing that the assassins feared?)
VI.  Conclusion

Question (b): The Message of Sophocles' *Antigone*

I.  Introduction
II.  The intellectual context of Classical Greece
III.  Sophocles' life and education
IV.  The message of the play
V.  The audience
VI.  Analysis
VII.  Conclusion

Question (c): Why did Alexander Kerensky fail?

I.  Introduction
II.  The historical context of Russia in the late 19th and early 20th century
III.  Kerensky's education and career
IV.  Russia and World War I
V.  The February Revolution
VI.  The provisional government and its policies
VII.  Lenin
VIII.  The October Revolution
IX.  Conclusion

Again, remember to cite primary sources as often as possible to support your points. While five pages may seem like a huge amount to a beginning college student, after you write a few such papers you will come to realize that it is just enough space to make a short, well-supported argument.

## **3.3**  Plagiarism

A critical lesson for writing any formal papers is to learn to avoid plagiarism. Indeed, recent investigations have shown that sometimes-famous historians even fall into this trap. Many students commit plagiarism without knowing what they have done.

At its simplest level, plagiarism is the use of someone else's work without attribution (from the Latin infinitive *plagiare*, to steal).

How do you avoid plagiarism? First and foremost, whenever you use the exact words of someone else (called a verbatim quotation) or a close rendering of what someone else wrote (called a paraphrase), cite the source either through a footnote, an endnote, or a parenthetical citation. The following section will show you how to approach citations.

In addition to verbatim quotations and paraphrases, you should cite information outside of the realm of "common knowledge." Students rightly ask where the border of common knowledge lies. Basically, common knowledge should include what you learned in a good high school history class. For instance, if you were writing a paper about the formation of the nation state of Bulgaria, you would not have to cite a general textbook source for stating that "Bulgaria is in southeast Europe" as a source for "World War I took place from 1914–1918." You would, however, need to cite the statement: "In late World War I, the Greek Prime Minister Venezelos launched a new front in Thessalonika that threatened Bulgaria."[1]

## 3.4   Citation of Sources

While the citation of sources is important to various disciplines, many have developed different standards and approaches to indicate where the author has found his or her information. So, a proper history paper will look very different from a sociology or psychology paper. Ultimately, you want to cite an author's name, the title of the work, and the relevant page numbers. To see the way historians normally accomplish this task, examine the standards set forth in *The Chicago Manual of Style*.[2] This style manual should be your ultimate resource. If you go on to

---

[1]   Barbara Jelavich, *A History of the Balkans: Twentieth Century* (Cambridge: Cambridge University Press, 1983), 120–121.

[2]   *The Chicago Manual of Style*, 14th ed. (Chicago: University of Chicago Press, 1993).

become a history or social studies secondary education major, you may want to purchase your own copy of the *Chicago Manual*.

Recently, a new type of citation, called the "author-date" form, is growing in popularity. With this method, the student gives the full bibliographic information either in a first note or in a bibliography,[3] and then gives a shortened citation of the author's name (with the date of publication following in parenthesis) followed by the relevant page numbers.[4] Students who work in more "highly specialized" areas of history will find that their subfields sometimes have slight variant stylistic conventions. Since style is something that is continually evolving, it is important to know that there are standards, but these standards tend to change over time. The growth in internet use has led to the creation of a style for citing web site sources. Remember that the ultimate goal is to be clear in your written expression and to include your sources.

While this text is not intended as a substitute for a style manual, but rather a short handbook to get first year students on their way, a few tips on the citation of sources follow.

a.  Footnotes and endnotes are different ways of achieving the same goal of showing your sources. With footnotes, the note appears at the bottom of the page. With endnotes, the notes are collected on a page (or pages) at the end of your paper. In the days when people wrote papers on typewriters, making footnotes was very complicated. There was a formula one used to subtract space from the bottom of a page for the text of each footnote. Endnotes were much easier. Now, with word processors and personal computers, it is no longer such a challenge to insert footnotes. Footnotes are preferable because the information is on the same page as the sentence where the citation is marked. Ask your instructor what he or

---

[3]  Example: Robert M. Frakes, *Contra Potentium Iniurias: The Defensor Civitatis and Late Roman Justice* (Munich: C. H. Beck Verlag, 2001).

[4]  Example: Frakes (2001), 197–203.

she prefers. If there is no preference, and if you have the "technology," go with footnotes.

b.  Number your notes consecutively—that is, start with 1 (one) and go on to 2 (two), and so on. In some other disciplines you move back and forth so 1 might appear several times. Don't do this for a history paper. There should be only one footnote number 1, number 2, and so on. Examine the examples on the preceding page.

c.  Always note direct quotations and paraphrases of primary sources (those sources from the time period under study).

d.  Likewise, always note direct quotations and paraphrases from secondary or tertiary sources (from writers later than the time period under study).

e.  Always try to work quotations in smoothly. That is, don't just stick the quotation in without some kind of lead in line (such as "Describing this, one historian has remarked …" or "Even contemporaries were impressed by his abilities. One witness recounted: …").

f.  If the quotation is shorter than three lines, double space it with normal margins and use quotation marks at the beginning and end of the quotation. If the quotation is longer than three lines, indent and single-space it, but omit the quotation marks.

g.  Cite sources for informative material outside of the realm of "common knowledge." Remember that our basic definition of "common knowledge" (which is becoming harder and harder to define as the diversity of our society becomes more and more acknowledged) is the material of a rigorous high school class. That is, you should not have to footnote a high school instructor's lecture material, but rather assume that what someone in the audience of a college class knows is "common knowledge."

h.  There used to be a list of Latin words and abbreviations that marked the serious student's work (*ibid, idem, op. cit., loc. cit., passim*). Most of these have fallen out of fashion in the ever-changing world of style. In this day and age it is probably best to avoid them. If the note is to a source you have cited before, cite it in a truncated way (such as "Buckler, 35."), with the appropriate page number.

## 3.5    The Internet as a Resource

With increasing internet availability and declining college library acquisition budgets, more and more students are using sources found on the internet as resources for research. While this topic will be dealt with more fully in the next chapter, keep in mind that not everything on the internet is true. Try to find out who the author is and what organization sponsors the web site. Also, be sure to avoid the temptation of "cutting and pasting" and not citing sources. This author has seen the number of cases of plagiarism rise dramatically with the availability of the internet. It is quite obvious to instructors when students insert a long section from another author. The change of style and voice exposes plagiarism. If the article is good, then cite it. If the source is questionable, don't use it. If the work is somewhat useful, paraphrase it and cite the source. (See the appendix on sample citations at the end of this handbook, page 52.)

## 3.6    Examples of Good and Bad Five-Page Papers

The following are two examples of five-page papers that might have been written for an upper-division history class. As you read through them, try to evaluate the papers in terms of the guidelines you have read. Do they have a clear structure? Is the grammar of the sentences clear? Do the papers have a solid argument? Do they include historical examples and citation of primary sources? Are they clear and convincing?

**Paper #1: "The USA and the Creation of Albania"**

*The Triple Entente (France and Russia—nation-states at the dawn of the twentieth century), among many others was created. They were vs. the triple Alliance (Germany, Austria-Hungary, Turkey, and Italy and a number of smaller nations). The two systems postulated rationally that they could not totally control*

*world Imperial systems. The creation of Albania took place be-
fore World War I began in 1914–1918.*

*The key factor was that nations in the Balkans (especially
the Serbians and the Bulgarians then) were fighting for territory
together with other lands of the time in Europe and elsewhere.
Conflicts developed into an economic crisis. All the nation states
of Europe and the Balkans argued about nationalism, histori-
cism, and the frontiers of their nation-states. Many hot spots
such as Transylvania, and the Sanjuk of Novi Pazar took place.
As a result of the Ottoman wars, Austria-Hungary first adminis-
tered and then seized the former military frontier. This made
many people both there, like Serbians, Albanians, and Sloveni-
ans, and elsewhere unhappy (just as today).*

*In reprisals, the Russians had plans, since Peter and Cath-
erine the Great, to support their desires for pan-slavism, ortho-
doxy, and warm-water ports by supporting the Balkan nations in
alliances that they hoped at the least in Europe, would support
the Habsburgs. On the other hand, the Habsburg government of
Austria seized parts of the government and administration of
parts of the former Ottoman Empire (a country in Europe)
around the time period of 1900. The Serbians, one of the
"Yugo" Slavs, desired to rebuild their greater Serbia (earlier
called Servia) of the Middle Ages (1389) throughout the Balkans
and asked their big Orthodox brother allies in Russia for help,
while the Habsburg empire hoped to gain the support of Germans for pan-slavism at the time in Europe. However, Russia
had lost a tremendous war against Japan (war), and was out of
the picture. Nationalism and Imperialism reared their ugly
heads because Serbia, in addition to other lands, would both
have claims to lands in Europe and elsewhere in the Aegean.*

*Several powers made a variety of various treaties to divide
and split up the Balkans for the balance of power earlier set up
at the Congress of Vienna in 1815 (at the end of the French
Revolution and Napoleon). In Russia, however, due to the last
war against Norway (1905), the Tsars, but also the Czars,
sought to try to attempt to maintain some territorial negotiations. The Russians and the Habsburg monarchy became cun-*

*ning and led to the Turks to follow these treaties were against their empire's lands and territories. Further treaties were made by Serbia, on the one hand, and Bulgaria (on the other)! Some ethnic groups in the European zone then felt cheated (IMRO and EMRO; see also the Ruthenians and the Galicians).*

*The more powerful governments in the time period (at the time period then) continued to have problems in the Balkans. The Bulgarian men and women felt because of economic and nationalistic reasons that they rationally needed a corridor to the seas. So, the Greeks wanted to take Thessaloniki. The Russian government tried to act rationally and efficiently; on the other hand, Turkey lost the war. This led to losing land and rational procedures in the Aegean. The Greeks now controlled the Aegean without Macedonia while the Italians, however, that is to say, in the "Mare Nostrum." The Greeks thus gained a "corridor to the sea" and Bulgarian men and women (especially in nationalistic sewing clubs) lost theirs. Italy gained further territory as the declining sick man of Europe lost it at that time. All this was the Turko-Italic war of 1911.*

*The nation-states soon watched with concern the situation in Southeastern Europe and decided to intervene but not really fight. They made everyone in Europe have a treaty, which would give the Balkan states control of the territories. The treaty was made in 1913 (and is one of the famous Treaties of London, in addition to the earlier one ending the American Revolution) and made Albania free.*

*The treaty changed Europe and the world. The Balkan states gained territories and lands and gave them those lands adjoining which was alot. The Turks gave Crete, part of the Aegean, to the Britains—a Balkan ally. Also, as stated earlier, Albania was made into an independent country in that time period, which was in Europe then, but would have a German king. Lastly, the so-called "great powers" would decide the face of the Aegean up to and including Mt. Blanc for all intensive purposes.*

*Woodrow Wilson, on the other hand, was born in the United States. He became president after William Howard Taft and Fighting Bob La Follette wanted to. He (Wilson) was a democ-*

*ratic who won more votes in the electoral college of representatives. Wilson's policy once he became president in 1913 was not on European affairs, but, on the contrary, was on American ones. The United States was not interested in Albania in that time period then. Indeed, they had never been, even since 1776, although Fan Noli was an Albanian bishop living in New York City who was elected by Albanian-Americans and had a vote in the Albanian parliament.*

*Later, World War I developed into Europe, and things changed over the course of the time period in which it was. Then Italy joined France, Great Britain and Russia in the Quadruple Alliance, against Germany, because the powers and because of the provinces of Ghent, Camucia, Trent, and Sasso Marconi and in this treaty, the pro-Slavism of Bulgaria, Russia, and Serbia was rebutted. This later treaty of London gave Italy more territory and this built nationalism at the time.*

*This all leads to some important conclusions. The creation of Albania was not successful in its attempt to force the two nation-states of the triple alliance to agree on land borders and frontiers in that time in the Balkans and elsewhere. This kind of nationalism led to a bloody conflict and long-lasting (that is to say, World War I). The agreement went against the Treaty to create World War I and, eventually, World War II.*

**Comments:** There are many problems with this paper. Indeed, it is difficult to say which is the biggest. Because you may not be a student of modern European history, I will not spend time on historical errors and instead will give a list of the more obvious structural problems:

1.  The paper has no central thesis. It is at some level about the creation of the country of Albania in the Treaty of London of 1913 (and without the title the reader might not know even that). But what about Albania? The author doesn't actually seem to know. It might conceivably be suggested that the thesis is that the creation of Albania in 1913 did not stop World War I from breaking out, but this thought is not clear

from the text of the paper. Since the author shifts to America later in the paper, and moreover uses "USA" in the title, might he or she instead be trying to argue that the Treaty of London was pleasing to Americans? Again, this is not developed. Remember to have a central argument clearly present in your introductory paragraph.

2.  The author cites no sources (primary or otherwise). A history paper must have citation of authorities and notes (footnotes or endnotes).

3.  The structure and development of this paper are very weak and unorganized. Part of the problem here may be that the author does not understand what is going on historically. Early in the paper the student should have defined why Albania was made a country (i.e., What war did it end? What were the opposing sides? What were the terms of the treaty?) and then developed the rest of the paper from there. As it is, the terms of the treaty that created the country appear very late in the paper, and the point of these terms of the treaty remains unclear.

4.  The sentence structure is terrible. Several sentences make no sense whatsoever. A few clunkers are: "In Russia, however, due to the last war against Norway (1905), the Tsars, but also the Czars, sought to try to attempt to maintain some territorial negotiations" or "Then Italy joined France, Great Britain and Russia in the Quadruple Alliance, against Germany, because the powers and because of the provinces of Ghent, Camucia, Trent, and Sasso Marconi and in this treaty, the pro-Slavism of Bulgaria, Russia, and Serbia was rebutted." Neither of these sentences makes sense either grammatically or historically. The author should review the earlier pages of this handbook.

## Paper #2: "The Eastern Crisis and Its Reception in the USA"

*The Great Eastern Crisis ending in 1878 was one of the most important developments in 19th century European History. Indeed, it brought Europe to the brink of the first wide-scale conflict since the Napoleonic Wars (which ended in 1815). Upon re-*

*examination of the origins and course of the Balkan Crisis to-*
*gether with the ensuing treaties, it becomes clear that the Great*
*European powers were becoming increasingly interested in the*
*Balkans—an interest that would lead to the outbreak of World*
*War I. Closer examination will show that Americans were origi-*
*nally little interested in these events which would ultimately lead*
*them some 36 years later into the "War to end all Wars" as*
*World War I became known.*

*The origins of the Crisis lie in the revolt of the Orthodox*
*Christian Bulgarians against the yoke of the oppressive Islamic*
*Ottoman Turks, who had controlled them since the late 14th cen-*
*tury.[1] The Bulgarians rose in the "April Uprising" of 1875, but*
*were then brutally suppressed in the "Bulgarian Horrors" in*
*which somewhere between 10,000 and 100,000 Bulgarians were*
*executed by the Turks, to the shock of Western Europeans and*
*Americans.[2] The Russians, both because of Pan-Slavism and*
*because they were co-religionists in the Orthodox Christian*
*faith, sent aid to their little Bulgarian brothers in April of 1877.[3]*
*As the Bulgarians and Russians began to have success against*
*the Turks, other Balkan peoples such as the Serbians and Greeks*
*also attacked the Ottomans. The combined Russian and Bulgar-*
*ian forces soundly defeated the Turks and in the Treaty of San*
*Stefano redrew the map of Southeastern Europe to reward Bul-*
*garia with a huge amount of land, access to the Sea, and also*
*gave the Russians a presence in this new Bulgaria for two*
*years.[4]*

*Many states were unhappy with the results of the Treaty of*
*San Stefano. Obviously, the Ottoman Empire did not like losing*
*territory. The Serbians and the Greeks felt they should have re-*
*ceived more territory. The great powers also were concerned*

---

[1]   Mercia Macdermott, *A History of Bulgaria: 1393–1885* (London: George
      Allen and Unwin, 1962), 15–235.

[2]   Macdermott, *A History of Bulgaria*, 275–286; Robert Lee Wolf, *The Balkans
      in Our Time* (New York: W. W. Norton and Co., 1967), 84.

[3]   Macdermott, *A History of Bulgaria*, 292–298.

[4]   Barbara Jelavich, *History of the Balkans: Eighteenth and Nineteenth Centu-
      ries* (Cambridge: Cambridge University Press, 1983), 352–359; Macdermott,
      *A History of Bulgaria*, 298–299; Wolf, *The Balkans*, 85.

with the large degree of new influence that Russia had gained, upsetting the Balance of Power set up by the Vienna Congress of 1815 in so far as Russia now had access to warm-water ports in the Eastern Mediterranean. Even the English were concerned that the Russian navy might now conceivably threaten the economic "life-line" of the British empire that flowed from India via the Suez canal (completed in 1869) to England.[5] There was apparently popular "jingoistic" support in England for war against Russia through popular epigrams such as the famous: "We don't want to fight, but by jingo, if we do, We've got the men, we've got the ships, we've got the money too!"[6]

Therefore, the great powers met in Berlin in June of 1878 to revise the Treaty of San Stefano. Representatives from the great powers as well as from the smaller Balkan states and from the Ottoman Empire were present. The great German chancellor Otto von Bismarck led the conference in the capital of the new German Empire. Mostly, the wishes of the Turks were ignored in favor of the desires of the majority of the great powers.

The Berlin Treaty greatly revised the Treaty of San Stefano and brought many changes to the boundaries of the Balkans. Bulgaria became autonomous from the Ottoman Empire. Serbia, Montenegro, and Rumania gained full independence as well as more land. Although there would be continuing problems bubbling under the surface, there would be no major political changes to the map of the Balkans after the Berlin Treaty of 1878 until the outbreak of the First Balkan War in 1912. Lastly, the power of Russia was greatly reduced in Bulgaria, thereby restoring the Balance of Power.[8]

The most dramatic achievement of the Treaty of Berlin was in revising the Treaty of San Stefano's treatment of Bulgaria,

[5]  Robert Gildea, *Barricades and Borders: Europe 1800–1914* (Oxford: Oxford University Press, 1987), 284.

[6]  Recorded in R. R. Palmer and Joel Colton, *A History of the Modern World since 1815*. 8th edition (New York: McGraw-Hill, 1995), 658.

[7]  Gildea, *Barricades and Borders*, 240–242; Wolf, *The Balkans*, 85.

[8]  Robin Okey, *Eastern Europe: 1740–1985*. 2nd Edition (Minneapolis: University of Minnesota Press, 1982), 133–134.

*especially in terms of size. What had been a "Greater" Bulgaria was cut up into smaller pieces and cut off from the eastern Mediterranean. Ultimately, the section which was the autonomous Bulgaria was about a third of the size of the Bulgaria set up by the Treatment of San Stefano.[9] Obviously, the Bulgarians and the Russians would be the most unhappy with this new treaty whereas the Serbians, Greeks, British, French, Germans, and Austrians would be happier with it.*

*Since this treaty, along with the revision of that of San Stefano, is so critical in both late 19th century history as well as leading up to the outbreak of World War I, it would seem plausible that there would be a large amount of reaction to it in the United States of America. Examining evidence of the "reception" of the treaty of Berlin might then lead us to understand ultimate American plans with regard to Europe in World War I. However, after reviewing a number of primary sources such as widely-read periodicals of the time like* Harper's Magazine *and* The New York Times, *it becomes clear that the issues leading to the Treaty of Berlin and the treaty itself were of little importance to Americans compared to domestic affairs.*

*For example, during the period from December of 1877 to May of 1879, there was no substantial article in* Harper's Magazine *that had anything to do with the Eastern Crisis of 1877–78. In contrast, in the period when this conflict took place, there was an article on the Eastern Shore of New Jersey which had 17 pages.[10] Another article spent eleven pages describing "The Normal College of New York City."[11] Therefore, the periodicals discussed subjects such as schools and landscape in America instead of events in Europe.*

*While coverage of the events in* Harper's *was slight, one would think that the* New York Times *might have had more up-to-date coverage. However, interestingly, the coverage in ar-*

---

[9]  Jelavich, *History of the Balkans*, 360–361.

[10]  William H. Rideing, "Along our Jersey Shore," *Harper's Magazine* 56 (1878), 321–338.

[11]  William H. Rideing, "The Normal College of New York City," *Harper's Magazine* 56 (1878), 672–683.

*guably America's greatest newspaper turns out, upon examination, to not differ much from that in* Harper's. *The events from the Balkans were only mentioned a few times during these events relating the terms of the Treaty of San Stefano, the unease in various countries of the terms of San Stefano, and reporting the boundaries as set by the Treaty of Berlin.[12]*

*While the* New York Times *gave some coverage, other widely read periodicals apparently did not report the events at all. It is intriguing that while the Great Powers of Europe were closely monitoring power shifts in the Balkans as the Ottoman Empire ("the Sick Man of Europe") declined further, Americans were seemingly not concerned as these events were so far away and of little interest. Americans of 1878 would have been shocked to learn that American troops would subsequently land in France in 1918 to take part in the largest war in world history up until that time ultimately as a result of Great Power interest in the Balkans.[13]*

**Comments:** This paper is clearly better than the first. The sentences and paragraphs are clear and the author cites both primary and secondary sources. The paper is not perfect, however. The thesis could be tightened a bit in the introductory paragraph to focus on why America is being brought into the paper. One way to do this would be to set up how many Americans served (or died) in World War I and then analyze backward from that to the Balkan crisis as an underlying cause. The author is anticipating this approach at the end of the concluding paragraph. As we have seen, in rough drafts the thesis often appears at the end of the paper because the author has finally figured out what the point of the paper should be. In this situation the student should revise the paper by moving the thesis to the beginning and reorganizing.

Also, the treatment of American periodicals could be handled more efficiently. The author clearly looked at some articles but casually cites many of them loosely together (especially

[12] *The New York Times* (1877–1879).
[13] Palmer and Colton, *A History of the Modern World*, 716.

from *The New York Times*). As a whole, the kind of primary source evidence that this paper uses can be classified as "negative" evidence. This is defined as a lack of coverage of a development in a primary source that may suggest something specific. Such an approach is certainly a kind of evidence, but "positive" evidence is much stronger ammunition to use. Whenever possible, use positive evidence that actually says something specific, rather than build an argument "from silence." The author should cast his or her net more widely and look into sources such as the *Congressional Record* and more politically oriented journals.

## <u>3.7</u>    Conclusion: Revising the Draft

You have now worked through the process of organizing and building a paper. The ideal way to approach writing a paper is to contemplate the sources, frame a thesis, compose a structure and outline, and then begin the writing process. After writing a draft, the key to good written expression is to revise your early drafts. In this process, you can first accomplish such obvious tasks as cleaning up typographical and grammatical errors. Then you can think about polishing the structure of your paper. Do you have the thesis in the first or second paragraph, or did you finally discover your thesis in the last two pages? Does your organization of examples flow logically, or should you reorder them?

# CHAPTER 4
## The Research Paper

A hallmark of advanced historical study at the undergraduate level, and indeed of a liberal arts education, is the research paper. Here the student encounters a wide body of information, reads widely until discovering a problem, defines a topic, and writes an extended argument over many pages that is supported by primary and secondary sources. The process of writing such a paper demands that the student delve deeply into library holdings and take accurate notes for subsequent formulation of the argument and for use as source citations.

The research paper draws upon all the skills taught in this handbook including structure, use of evidence, and clarity of argument. A student's involvement in such an exercise is not only the culmination of undergraduate education, but it also provides useful skills in the workplace where one may well have to research a problem and write a report, regardless of profession. This section will guide you through the process of choosing and defining a topic, conducting research, using sources, and organizing and writing the paper. It will end with an examination of sample introductions and conclusions of research papers.

## 4.1 Types of Papers

The types of assignments mentioned earlier in this handbook all lead toward the research paper. The identification paragraph requires that students show what they know in a limited and structured way. The essay requires that students show what they know, but through an argumentative form where possible. The five-page paper requires that students make an argument, but its length limits how long and detailed this argument can be.

Traditionally, students were taught that there were three kinds of writing: narrative, descriptive, and expository. A narrative composition involves the telling of a story. The "trace the developments leading to ..." type of essay question would fall under the rubric of narrative. A descriptive composition, as the name implies, describes something such as a place or an object. While various kinds of fiction and nonfiction use description, many students' essays and papers fall into a blend of narrative and descriptive. In an expository composition, the writer makes an argument. As we have seen earlier, the best kind of five-page paper is one that is framed as an argument, or an expository composition. This approach is even more critical for research papers. So, the ideal research paper will be an expository piece, which will include narrative and descriptive elements.

How long should a research paper be? This is a difficult question. Many instructors will answer "as long as it takes to make an effective argument that is well-supported by sources." This answer, of course, does not help a student new to history research papers. This author usually tells students to aim for 10 to 15 pages, but not to worry if it grows beyond that limit. Realize, however, that some instructors expect at least 25 pages (following the philosophy that students learn to write by writing a lot!). The best answer to the question of length is to ask your instructor what he or she expects. If the instructor does not give a clear answer, ask what length most "A" papers seem to have. Regardless of the potential length, the good research paper will have a focused thesis, will be supported by evidence and examples, and will have a clear organization.

## 4.2    Defining the Topic

One of the most challenging initial parts of writing a research paper is defining the topic. A good topic allows the author the opportunity to make an extended argument based on primary sources, and, at some level, to also treat interpretations in secondary sources. Obviously, establishing a good topic is difficult to do immediately, so it is best to work toward this goal in stages. First, you need to find an **area** of interest. An area could be a time period (i.e., Medieval Europe), an event (i.e., World War

II), or a process (i.e., Western relations with Imperial China). Then, you need to start reading broadly, in textbooks at first, and then in more specialized works, to find an aspect of that area that is especially interesting and also has the feel of a "problem" that you can engage. When reading widely, check the bibliography at the ends of chapters and books to track down further resources.

While conducting further research in some of these resources, keep your mind open for any problems of interpretation. You will discover that scholars have differences of interpretation over sources and events. Such a difference of opinion or debate will provide a good way to approach the material. When you find a potential topic, discuss it with your instructor. So, while we started with broad areas like Medieval Europe, World War II, or Western relations with Imperial China, after wide reading and discussion with an instructor, we might end up with topics such as "The Evolution of the Drawbridge in Castles in Medieval Wales," or "The Depiction of World War II in African-American Newspapers from 1941–1945," or "The British Government's View of the Opium Trade in China (1839–1840)." Not only are these topics more focused and detailed than the broad areas, but they also suggest the kind of primary source data with which the students might work (i.e., physical remains of castles, African-American newspapers, or British government documents). Think of the process of identifying a research paper topic as being similar in design to a funnel: it is very broad at the top, but as you read more widely, the topic focuses more and more.

### Good and Bad Topics

The process of identifying the topic is the critical first step in writing the research paper. If you don't have a focused topic, and you don't have primary sources on which to base your research, your paper is doomed. Examine the following titles of papers and evaluate whether or not they are good research topics. (Keep in mind that the role of the title is both to grab the reader's interest and to state the topic clearly at the very beginning of the paper.)

"The Story of the Destruction of the Kulaks"

"Witches in Early Modern Europe"

"What has Athens to do with Missouri?: The Greek Civil War and the Truman Doctrine"

"Critias of Athens: Oligarchic Reactionary or Democratic Radical?"

"Out of the Loop?: The USA and the Creation of Albania"

"Early Colonial Guatemala"

"The Development of the Steamship and the USA's Annexation of Hawaii"

You probably noticed that some of these seem to be very broad topics verging on an "area" while others clearly suggest a focused topic. Thus, "The Story of the Destruction of the Kulaks," "Witches in Early Modern Europe," and "Early Colonial Guatemala" all appear to be narrative or descriptive papers. The more focused papers ("What has Athens to do with Missouri?: The Greek Civil War and the Truman Doctrine," "Critias of Athens: Oligarchic Reactionary or Democratic Radical?," "Out of the Loop?: The USA and the Creation of Albania," and "The Development of the Steamship and the USA's Annexation of Hawaii") all suggest a process of research and focused thought that leads to good, provocative research topics.

## 4.3   Using Primary and Secondary Sources

We have seen earlier in this handbook that primary sources (sources actually from the time period under study) are the most powerful kind of evidence to use in historical writing. This rule holds for research papers also. Primary sources for a research paper might include literary sources (such as histories, diaries, magazines, newspapers, novels, and poems), documentary sources (laws, treaties, numerical data like census figures), or material remains (such as archaeological evidence).

You will also want to examine secondary sources in the research paper. Secondary sources are works written after an event by historians or biographers who are trying to interpret the event based upon primary sources. For the purposes of your research paper, secondary sources would include books, articles, and book reviews by scholars. Such works will help you define your topic further because you will find disagreements of interpretation in them, and you might find some arguments more interesting than others. Published book reviews in scholarly journals (such as the *American Historical Review*, *The Historian*, or others that your instructor may recommend) may give you some useful ideas about how to revise arguments laid out in books and monographs. Check *Book Review Digest* for references to major book reviews.

## Research in the Library

While reading in textbooks and following up bibliographic references are good beginnings to your research, you will find that you must use the resources of your college library effectively to accumulate the critical mass of primary and secondary source material necessary to write an effective paper. There are several reference guides available (probably in the reference room of your library) to aid in historical research which will help you find secondary sources. In turn, the secondary sources, if they are sound, should cite primary sources in their notes. For topics in American history, examine the indices of *America: History and Life* (Santa Barbara: ABC-Clio) which currently has over 450,000 entries. For topics in world history since 1450, search through *Historical Abstracts* (Santa Barbara: ABC-Clio) which has over 600,000 entries.

Most academic libraries also have search engines available to students (often via the library's home page on the internet). Through such databases as "EBSCO" and others, students can gain further access to a wide body of secondary literature. In beginning your library research, consult one of the reference librarians at your institution about your working topic and be sure to ask what printed and computer-based reference works are available.

Not to be ignored is the old-fashioned approach of "walking the stacks." Before elaborate databases existed, and even before many printed reference sources were available, college students found that an effective way of doing historical research was to look up key words relating to their topic in the library catalog and then to search the shelf of the library where those call numbers appeared. In addition to the book discovered in the catalog, look at books to the right and the left of it on surrounding shelves and browse through the tables of contents, indices, endnotes/footnotes, and bibliographies for information related to your topic. Some of the best insights can occur from examining related works.

## Note Cards

When conducting research with library materials, it is imperative to note key arguments and quotations that might be helpful in writing your paper. While you will not know for certain whether every single quotation will be important, by the time you are leafing through works in the library aisles, you probably have some idea as to whether something may be remotely useful. Put a slip of paper in the book to mark the page and write down the passage and related thoughts you have as soon as possible.

Students long ago discovered that noting such passages on 3 × 5 inch cards was a good tactic. While you could use sheets of paper or a laptop computer for notes, the advantage to note cards is that you have a separate card for each important citation. Be sure to note the bibliographic reference for each passage, so you can cite it adequately in the writing of your paper. When you reach the stage of actually formulating the structure of your argument, you can play out variant approaches by lining up the note cards in different arrangements. This author remembers resorting to the floor of my dorm room as a display surface to layout different alternatives for my paper's structure because my desk top wasn't big enough. Once you have a good working structure, write your outline with references to the respective note cards.

## Types of Citations

Because of the large number of primary and secondary sources you will examine, your research paper will naturally have many notes citing sources (and your instructor will expect it to). If it does not, your topic, research approach, and/or source material available may be problematic. You may want to rethink your paper, and discuss options with your instructor.

For citing sources, follow the rules suggested in the five-page paper section in Chapter 3 as well as the Appendix on Citations at the end of this handbook. Keep in mind that a research paper may have other kinds of notes in addition to the classic note that cites a primary or secondary source. These include descriptive and provocative notes. The descriptive, or textual, note is for information which you may have discovered through the course of your research that is interesting and somewhat useful, but tangential to your argument.[1] If you had the information in the text of your paper it might distract the reader, but in a note you can still use it effectively. In a similar fashion, the provocative note is useful for ideas that have occurred to you in examining primary or secondary sources that, while not directly germane to your argument, are insights that you would like to share. Occasionally, some very creative ideas emerge out of such notes.

## 4.4   The Internet as a Resource

As you no doubt know, the internet is becoming more and more important as a resource for all kinds of research. This is especially the case for history students at colleges with smaller libraries. Through intelligent and effective use of the internet,

---

[1] Example: It is interesting that writing guides and handbooks from the 1950s gave concrete evidence and examples, while works from the 1970s and 1980s moved away from such practical advice.

students can access both primary and secondary sources not easily available through local collections.

As you might also know, in addition to some very useful sources, there is a great deal of "garbage" on the internet that ranges from totally useless material, to that which is downright wrong, unsubstantiated, biased, and/or hate-filled. Naturally, you want to use the good sources, and not the bad, in writing your paper. For a student beginning the research process, differentiating the former from the latter is not always easy. One hint is to lean toward "edu" and "org" addresses over "com," "net," and other domains. "Edu" signifies an accredited institution of higher learning in the United States. Often you can find web sites created by professors who are specialists in their fields. However, "edu" sites also may include college student work which varies significantly in its quality and accuracy. Be careful to find out who the author or compiler of the site is. "Org" signifies a nonprofit organization. Many of these sites are scholarly and well-documented. However, some "org" addresses are non-scholarly (and some of the organizations might even be classified as hate groups, so be sure to learn who has authored or compiled the web site). It proves useful to move from the web page that may have initially appeared as a search engine result (i.e., Yahoo!, Altavista, Google, etc.) to the home page for that respective web site. On the home page you can find more information about the person or organization sponsoring the source. If the sponsor is an association of professional historians at various well-known universities, the site is probably more valid than a site created by someone claiming to have been kidnapped by aliens.

As stated earlier, be careful about lifting information directly from an internet source to your paper. While this might seem quick and easy, the author is not trying to make the same argument you are, and the change in style and voice will suggest plagiarism to your instructor.

## Some Useful Internet Sites

Here is a list of scholarly web sites for different subgroups of professional historians which may provide useful links for your research. If any of these sites appears to be a potential area for your research, navigate around the site and look for further links and resources. Keep in mind that internet addresses change, and new scholarly web sites are created frequently. If these particular examples don't work, you may have to plug the name of the association into a search engine.

Association of Ancient Historians
   **(www.trentu.ca/ahc/aah/welcome.shtml)**

Encyclopedia of Roman Emperors
   **(www.roman-emperors.org)**

American Society for Eighteenth-Century Studies
   **(www.asecs.press.jhu.edu)**

American Society for Environmental History
   **(www2.h-net.msu.edu/~environ/membership.html)**

American Society of Church History
   **(www.churchhistory.org)**

Committee on Lesbian and Gay History
   **(www.usc.edu/isd/archives/clgh)**

Conference on Latin American History
   **(www.h-net.msu.edu/~clah/)**

Renaissance Society of America
   **(www.r-s-a.org)**

Society for Historians of the Early American Republic
   **(www2.h-net.msu.edu/~shear/)**

Society for Historians of the Gilded Age and Progressive Era
   **(www.h-net.msu.edu/~shgape)**

World War Two Studies Association
   **(www2.h-net.msu.edu/~war/wwtsa/)**

Society for Historians of American Foreign Relations
   **(www.shaff.history.ohio-state.edu/)**

## <u>4.5</u>    Structure and Organization

While the structure of the essay, and even of the five-page paper, is simple enough to lay out without knowing the particulars of the topic and of the sources, giving a general statement on the structure and organization of a research paper is more difficult. Every research paper is fundamentally different because of the nature of the process of defining the topic, working with the sources, and laying out an argument. There are, however, some basic elements of structure that must still be stressed for a research paper:

a.    Write an introduction. This first paragraph or two should introduce the reader to the topic and to your thesis. It may be that your introduction will take more than one or, in special circumstances, more than two paragraphs.

b.    Give some background (or context) to your topic. You will want to do this in a couple of paragraphs. Be careful not to let it overwhelm your reader early in the paper and muddy your topic. By using topic and concluding sentences well in these paragraphs, you will be able to keep the reader on track.

c.    Develop your interpretation of primary and secondary sources well. Your reader will especially be looking for this interpretation in your paper. Here is where effective organization of your note cards will pay dividends. After several pages of such examination, you will want to build your analysis in greater detail.

d.    Lastly, have a solid concluding paragraph (or two or three) where you detail the significance of your research and present your conclusion.

## <u>4.6</u>    Rules for Layout or Appearance

While we began to discuss the physical appearance of a history paper in the last chapter, since the research paper is longer and is seen as a more formal piece of composition, the lay out will be even more important. Make sure to comply with your instructor's rules or suggestions. Ultimately, your paper will have three to four parts:

1. *Title Page.* Try to think of a title that grabs the reader's attention and demonstrates that your work is an analysis of a problem, rather than a summary or a narrative. The title of your paper should be centered, about one-fourth of the way down from the top. Type your name below the title and center it as well. About one-third of the way up from the bottom, type the course number and title, the instructor's name, and the date on separate lines.

2. *Text of the Paper.* The text should be double-spaced and should run anywhere from 10 to 25 pages. (Again, check with your instructor even before you begin doing research so that you have an idea of the scale of your presentation.) Use a 12-point font such as New York or Times. Most people still prefer the old-fashioned look of the uneven right margin or "ragged right." Speaking of margins, try to follow the traditional approach of having 1.25 inch margins for the left and right margins and 1 inch margins for the top and bottom (or "headers" and "footers"). Be sure to have a page number in the upper-right corner (after the title page). Try to avoid "widow" and "orphan" lines (single lines of text, such as the first or last lines of a paragraph) at the top or bottom of a page.

   If your instructor doesn't have a specific preference, decide whether to have footnotes (at the bottom of each page) or endnotes (at the end of all your pages of text). If you are working with a good word-processing program, and making footnotes is just as simple as making endnotes, go for the footnotes. This way, the text or citation is handy for the reader and he or she won't have to keep flipping back and forth. If you are using footnotes, skip the next section and go straight to the bibliography.

3. *Endnotes.* If you have decided to use endnotes, (this section will follow the body of your paper) type a centered subtitle

("Notes") at the top of the page and then number your notes consecutively.

4. *Bibliography.* Your last section should be the bibliography. Center this term as your subtitle. List all the primary and secondary sources you consulted in the writing of your paper. Some instructors prefer that you compile a "Select Bibliography" where a full citation is given for any work that has been cited in the notes more than once. Ask your instructor which approach he or she would prefer. For bibliography style, check Appendix 3 on page 54 of this handbook.

## <u>4.7</u>    Conclusion: Revising the Research Paper

While the last chapter gave some preliminary remarks on revising a five-page paper, this section will treat the topic of revising a research paper in more depth. Often, students work on research papers in history courses classified as "seminars." The history seminar was the creation of the German scholar Leopold von Ranke in the early nineteenth century at the University of Berlin. In his concept of a seminar, students would work on research projects using primary sources under the direction of a professor, report on the progress of their work, and write up their results. History seminars in American universities follow this model fairly closely.

An important part of the seminar experience is to have the instructor and the other students "critique" a given student's work in progress (either an oral report, or even more importantly, a written draft). At the outset, students should keep in mind that the purpose of this exercise is to improve the student's methodology and to improve the paper (and thus to improve the grade the student will receive). Remember, there is a difference between "critiquing" (pointing out problems that can be improved and how to improve them) and "criticizing." If you are in this situation, try to be helpful to your fellow students. Give them the kind of good advice that you yourself would appreciate receiving (and try to give it in a manner that you would appreciate). Remember also, the time will come when you will be the one receiving a critique.

Sometimes, to start off a critiquing session, an instructor will ask you to give a five-to-fifteen-minute presentation about your own (or someone else's) paper. If you are going to make such a presentation, plan out what you are going to say, practice it, and time it. Give the broad context for the area of history, state the thesis of the paper, and present the organization the paper follows, the kind of sources the paper uses, and the significance of the results.

## A Check List for Revisions

\_\_\_\_ Does your title catch the reader's interest and pertain to your paper?

\_\_\_\_ Is your thesis in the first one or two paragraphs of your paper?

\_\_\_\_ Does your introduction match the paper you have written?

\_\_\_\_ Did you follow through on your thesis?

\_\_\_\_ Can you refine your thesis (after rereading your paper)?

\_\_\_\_ Do you adequately cite your sources in notes?

\_\_\_\_ Do you cite primary and secondary sources?

\_\_\_\_ Do you have balanced examples?

\_\_\_\_ Do the first sentences of each paragraph suggest what each paragraph will be about?

\_\_\_\_ Have you cleaned up typographical errors?

\_\_\_\_ Have you cleaned up grammatical errors?

\_\_\_\_ Have you had a friend proofread the paper to catch additional errors?

\_\_\_\_ Have you given yourself time to revise?

\_\_\_\_ How can you make your paper better?

## **4.8** Examples of Introductions and Conclusions of Research Papers

The following examples show the introductions and conclusions to three research papers for an upper-division class on the history of the Roman Empire. The only direction for research was to "find a problem in a primary source for the Roman Empire." As you read through the introductions, ask yourself how clearly developed the thesis is and how well organized the paper seems. I have also included the concluding paragraphs for comparison and contrast with the introductions. Comments for improvement will follow each sample. Try to gauge which example is the best in terms of clarity of thesis.

## 1. "Ammianus Marcellinus: The Last Roman Historian"

**Introduction** *In studying a historian of a period so remote in time and culture from ours such as the fourth century A.D. Ammianus Marcellinus, one must try to appreciate the way that he might have viewed the world in order to read his history fairly. By this, one tries to read history as the author, Ammianus, wanted it to be read. This process yields, at the very least, three products. First, one gains insight into the life and thought of an ancient author and what his political and social worlds were. Second, one sees a detailed narrative of a decisive time in western history. This account is the most complete source on the period from the death of Constantine to the death of Valens in 378. This historical period saw the establishment of Christianity as the firm religion of the Roman world as well as the inroads of Gothic invaders into the Roman state that was destined to collapse from their effect. Third, one gains self-knowledge. For in critically analyzing and attempting to re-create the world of a historian writing over a millennium and a half ago, one changes inwardly. One's own historical conceptions, mind set, and world view cannot help but be changed. This is not to say that one would adopt the world view of a certain fourth-century man. Rather, by critically examining his work, by trying to abandon early twenty-first century values and preconceptions to see him clearly, those same values and preconceptions will be altered. This process cannot help but be ever continuing. Thus, the view of history and historical men, as well as the conceptions of one's own history will be continually growing and continually evolving as one studies history.*

**Conclusion** *Ammianus saw that the traditional Roman values of Fortune and Virtue had become alienated from each other in the fourth-century Roman world. His message was a warning to the cultivated aristocracy of that state. The twin threats of internal decadence and external invasions of Germans and Persians were going to overcome the Roman state if something was not done. Ammianus presents the image of the Emperor Julian as a prototype of correct conduct, of a possible return to greatness and strength. By accepting responsibility for the Roman state, by cultivating traditional Roman virtues, the aristocracy could save the Roman world from the impending disaster (in Ammianus' eyes). Virtue and Fortune could be realigned and the Roman state could return to its rightful position in the world. To this end, Ammianus Marcellinus, an ethnic Greek of the Roman state, fought in its army for over ten years, and wrote this moral history, this last Roman history, as a further defense of his world.*

**Comments:** A close reading of these two paragraphs shows that the author does not reach his or her thesis until the conclusion. In the rather long and sweeping introduction, the author attempts to be philosophical about the purpose of studying history (and at some level it is an endearing attempt). However, the conclusion doesn't match the introduction. In the conclusion we come upon what has clearly evolved as a thesis in the paper—the purpose of Ammianus' history. The author should purge the second half of the introductory paragraph and instead anticipate what the focus of the paper will be.

## 2. "Eunapius of Sardis: Historian and Historical Controversy"

**Introduction** *Eunapius of Sardis is a frequently disputed source for the later Roman Empire. Scholars from the Byzantine lexicographer Photius onward have presented different theories regarding Eunapius and the nature of his work. Eunapius, a fourth-century pagan historian, wrote two (or perhaps three) works. The only one extant is his* Lives of the Philosophers and

Sophists. *The other one or two were of a political/ historical nature. This political history (hereafter the* Universal History) *is preserved only in fragments in Byzantine compilations and in other authors' works. When one tries to read Eunapius, one finds himself inevitably drawn into the fascinating world of secondary scholarship that analyzes Eunapius'* Quellenforschung *(German for "Source Research").*

**Conclusion** *In the midst of all this heady research, one is apt to lose sight of the simplest facts of a problem. Eunapius, as far as we know, lived in Sardis from 369 until his death in c. 414. Ammianus, on the other hand, probably lived and wrote in the city of Rome in the western part of the empire around 400. We have seen that many scholars have argued Eunapius read Ammianus' history (written c. 388–395) and based his history (which was written anywhere from 378–393) upon that earlier work. However, this theory is not necessarily true. The publication process of the late Roman world was not as instantaneous as our own. Moreover, the work of Oribasius, who we have seen was a doctor who accompanied Julian and wrote an account (now lost) of his war against Persia, may not have influenced either Eunapius or Ammianus. Ammianus also accompanied Julian's expedition and probably based his account upon his own experiences. Since there are so many lines of demarcation between these works, and because the chronology is so unclear, it is safest to assume that Eunapius and Ammianus wrote independently of each other (and probably of Oribasius) in describing a tumultuous period of Roman history.*

**Comments:** The introduction of this second paper is more succinct and to some degree more clear than the first, but the author is also cagier. He or she hints that a thesis will be emerging in the course of the paper ("the reader finds himself... drawn into... secondary scholarship") without actually explaining what the thesis will be. Again, only in the conclusion do we discover that the key problem is the interrelationship of the work of Eunapius with that of Ammianus, and here the author ultimately argues that they wrote independently of each other. So far, this paper is a good draft, but it could be revised by moving the thesis to the introduction and re-examining the subsequent organization of the paper.

### 3. "A Study of Documentary Papyri from the Reign of Elagabalus"

**Introduction** *Since the late nineteenth century, the discovery of Egyptian papyri has contributed greatly to our knowledge of ancient history. Whereas before that point we had only literary sources and some inscriptions for knowledge of ancient Roman administration, now we have many official documents that shed light on how a Roman province was governed and upon social life in the ancient world. One particular use of documentary papyri is to use it to compare and contrast with traditional literary sources to evaluate the reigns of Roman emperors. Few Roman emperors match up to the image of Elagabalus (who reigned from 218–222) for sheer depravity in traditional literary sources like that of Herodian, Dio Cassius, and the anonymous* Historia Augusta. *However, re-examination of the documents surviving on papyrus in the province of Egypt, if not exactly contradicting the traditional sources, demonstrates that for the average Roman in the provinces life went on relatively unchanged no matter who was emperor.*

**Conclusion** *Was Elagabalus an insane "catamite" or a religious political theorist? The papyri cannot tell us. However, documents surviving from the sands of Egypt can tell us that the emperor's behavior did not rock the empire, only the senators whose position he ignored. Augustus' provincial apparatus ran on with even inexperienced favorites of the ruler as political appointees, just as some agencies do in some modern countries. Thus, the papyri serve to illustrate problems and gaps in the literary sources of antiquity and to shed even more light on how the common man lived in the provinces of the Roman Empire.*

**Comments:** Here the student has clearly worked through an earlier draft and revised his or her paper. We see a clear, focused thesis at the end of a succinct first introductory paragraph. We can imagine that, in the rest of the paper, the student laid out the standard traditional descriptions of the emperor's reign, followed by a description of the contents of surviving documents on papyri. The conclusion draws the reader into the wider significance of such an argument.

# APPENDIX 1
## Common Mistakes

The following is a list of mistakes in writing that this author has often noticed over the course of 15 years of grading student assignments. Try to read them over before beginning the process of writing your essay or papers. If you are writing a formal research paper, it might serve you well to reread them before proofreading your paper during the revision process.

Lack of clarity.

Lack of structure.

Lack of evidence.

Absence of notes and citations.

Lack of time budgeting. This too often means the first part of an essay is swimming in so much detail that all the major points are lost, and the second part of the essay is pathetically thin.

One-sentence paragraphs.

Overly-long paragraphs with too many disparate topics included.

Paragraphs with no topic sentences.

Indenting at the tops of pages when in the middle of a sentence or paragraph.

Incomplete sentences without subject, verb, or object.

Run-on sentences.

Subject-verb agreement (he is, they were; not he were, they is).

Consistency in tenses. ("The treaty was a temporary agreement that did not solve the problem." rather than "The treaty is a temporary agreement that did not solve the problem.")

Sweeping generalizations (including inaccurate statements that have nothing to do with either lectures or the textbook) with no support from evidence or examples.

Use of the first person in formal writing such as identification paragraphs or essays (i.e., avoid sentences starting with "I feel ..." or "I think ..." or "It seems to me ...").

The apostrophe s ('s). Use it for possession, not to make nouns plural! That is, "Alexander the Great's conquests" not "The Roman's had many conquests."
   The stylistic jury is still out on whether to use a simple apostrophe or an apostrophe s when denoting possession of nouns that end in -s. So either Julius' or Julius's is acceptable.

"Their" vs. "There."

"Its" vs. "It's."

"Where" vs. "were."

"Alot" vs. "A lot."

"Would've" = "would have," not "would of."

Spelling. If you are using a word processing computer, use the spell check and grammar check programs.

# APPENDIX 2
## Sample Citations

Here are examples of the most common types of notes you might use in writing five-page or research papers. Read them over to get a feel for how to write citations of sources. Find the appropriate example when you are writing your papers. If you cannot find the type of note you need here, you should consult the *Chicago Manual of Style*.

### Primary Sources

1. Citation of Primary Source—Book:
   George Orwell, *1984* (New York: Harcourt, Brace, 1949).

2. Citation of Primary Source—Article:
   William H. Rideing, "The Normal College of New York City," *Harper's Magazine* 56 (1878), 672–683.

3. Citation of Primary Source within Edited Collection:
   *Priscus of Panium, An Embassy to the Huns*, ed. and trans. James H. Robinson, *Readings in European History* (Boston: Ginn and Company, 1904), vol. 1, 30–33, following C. W. Hollister, Joe W. Leedom, Marc A. Meyer, and David S. Spear, eds., *Medieval Europe: A Short Sourcebook*, 2d ed. (New York: McGraw Hill, 1992), 20–21.

4. Citation of Primary Source from Internet Site:
   Sir Francis Bacon, *The New Atlantis*
   (**http://www.perseus.org**); accessed July 8, 2002.

### Secondary Sources

1. Citation of Secondary Source—Book:
   Crane Brinton, *The Anatomy of Revolution* (New York: Prentice Hall, 1952).

Robert M. Frakes, *Contra Potentium Iniurias: The Defensor Civitatis and Late Roman Justice* (Munich: C. H. Beck Verlag, 2001).

2. Citation of Secondary Source—Article:
   Frank J. Frost, "Akakallis, a Divinity of Western Crete," *Ancient World* 27 (1996), 53–58.

3. Citation of Secondary Source from Edited Collection:
   David L. Toye, "Plutarch on Poetry, Prose, and Politeia," in *The Dance of Hippocleides: A Festschrift for Frank J. Frost*, ed. Robert M. Frakes and David L. Toye (Golden, CO: Ares Publishers, 2002), 173–181.

4. Citation of Secondary Source from Internet Site:
   Michael DiMaio, Jr., "Maxentius (306–312 A.D.)," *De Imperatoribus Romanis* (**http://www.roman-emperors.org/maxentiu.htm**), 1–3; accessed July 8, 2002.

# APPENDIX 3

## Sample Bibliography

Here are the major types of entries you will use in writing the bibliography for your five-page or research papers. Read them over to get a feel for how to write such entries. Find the appropriate example when you are writing your papers.

### Primary Sources

1. Primary Source—Book:
   Orwell, George. *1984*. New York: Harcourt, Brace, 1949.

2. Primary Source—Article:
   Rideing, William H. "The Normal College of New York City," *Harper's Magazine* 56 (1878), 672–683.

3. Primary Source from Internet Site:
   Bacon, Sir Francis. *The New Atlantis* (**http://www.perseus.org**); accessed July 8, 2002.

### Secondary Sources

1. Secondary Source—Book:
   Brinton, Crane. *The Anatomy of Revolution*. New York: Prentice Hall, 1952.
   Frakes, Robert M. *Contra Potentium Iniurias: The Defensor Civitatis and Late Roman Justice*. Munich: C. H. Beck Verlag, 2001.

2. Secondary Source—Article:
   Frost, Frank J. "Akakallis, A Divinity of Western Crete," *Ancient World* 27 (1996), 53–58.

3.  Secondary Source from Edited Collection:
    Toye, David L. "Plutarch on Poetry, Prose, and Politeia," in
    *The Dance of Hippocleides: A Festschrift for Frank J. Frost*,
    ed. Robert M. Frakes and David L. Toye, 173–181. Golden,
    CO: Ares Publishers, 2002.

4.  Secondary Source from Internet Site:
    DiMaio, Michael J., Jr. "Maxentius," *De Imperatoribus Ro-
    manis*  (**http://www.roman-emperors.org/maxentiu.htm**),
    1–3; accessed July 8, 2002.

# APPENDIX 4
## Classic History Essay Questions

The following list is made up of typical history essay questions drawn from survey courses in Western Civilization, World Civilization, and U.S. History. It is based on the author's own experience and contributions from colleagues at a variety of institutions (regional state universities, private liberal arts colleges, and community colleges).

While the list is no guarantee of what will show up on the student's examination, it will provide an idea of the scale of importance of what might appear and provide different approaches one can take in organizing responses. Look through the list of questions for the type of course you are taking, and contemplate how you might approach an essay question that covers material you have learned. Also, think about how you might structure your response in terms of the number of paragraphs and what kinds of examples and evidence you would use to support your argument.

### Western/World Civilization:

1. Which was more important in the early civilizations (c. 3000–800 B.C.E.) we have examined so far—technology or religion?

2. To what extent have modern scholars changed the traditional view of early history?

3. If you had to choose only five major pieces of evidence to best explain the history of Early Western Civilization from 8000–500 B.C.E., what would you choose and why?

4. Why did the Romans, and not the Greeks, successfully conquer the Mediterranean World?

5. Choose five authors of primary sources that best explain Early Western Civilization from c. 800 B.C.E.–100 A.D./C.E.

6. Choose five individuals (they can be historical people or literary characters from primary sources) who best explain important developments in Early Western Civilization from c. 800 B.C.E.–100 A.D./C.E.

7. In 64 A.D./C.E., Peter and Paul were martyred in the city of Rome by the emperor Nero. However by 1100 A.D., bishops of Rome were dictating foreign and domestic policy to kings. How did this change come about?

8. In 390 A.D., the Mediterranean World was still rule by a unified Roman Empire. By 750, the political map of the Mediterranean looked very different. Explain the differences.

9. If you had to select only five primary sources to explain the most important developments in the history of Western Civilization from c. 100–1200 A.D./C.E., what would they be and why?

10. What was more important, the Renaissance or the Reformation? Give examples and evidence and be sure to examine both.

11. In the first half of the nineteenth century, the Balkan nations were secondary to European great power interest. In 1914, however, they were the cause of the "Great War." Explain this transformation.

12. Compare and contrast the Vienna Congress and the Paris Peace Conference of 1919.

13. Choose five authors who best exemplify changing ideas from the mid-nineteenth century to the mid-twentieth century. Justify your choices.

14. What killed more people in the 20th century: ideology or the machine gun?

## U.S. History:

1. What motivated people more to settle in the American colonies, the desire for economic opportunity or the desire for religious freedom? Support your answer with examples.

2. Discuss the ways in which historical development (i.e., wars, revolutions, political struggles, and economic hardship) in Europe and Africa shaped the course of history in the original 13 colonies from their foundation to 1763.

3. If you were to arrive in the American colonies in the late 1600s, what groups of people would you expect to find there? Which groups settled where, and with what goals?

4. What were the origins of the American Revolution?

5. What were the strengths and weaknesses of the Constitution when it was written? Be sure to think about what events came before and afterwards in American history.

6. Trace the developments leading to the outbreak of the Civil War.

7. Why did the North win the Civil War?

8. What were the three most important developments in American history from the end of the Civil War to America's entry into World War I?

9. Why did the U.S.A. enter World War I?

10. What was the effect of the Great Depression on the United States?

11. What was the effect of World War II on the United States?

12. What was the effect of the Cold War on the United States?

13. Describe the five most important developments in U.S. history since the end of the Civil War.

14. If you could choose only five people from American history (from the colonial period to the present) to best explain the nation's history to you, which five would you choose and why?